Edited by
ANDREW ROBERTS
NEIL JOHNSON
and **TOM MILTON**

BIBLICAL TEACHING

66 They devoted themselves
to the apostles' teaching and to
fellowship, to the breaking
of bread and to prayer. 99

The Bible Reading Fellowship
15 The Chambers, Vineyard
Abingdon OX14 3FE
brf.org.uk

The Bible Reading Fellowship (BRF) is a Registered Charity (233280)

ISBN 978 0 85746 678 5
First published 2018
10 9 8 7 6 5 4 3 2 1 0

Acknowledgements
Unless otherwise acknowledged, scripture quotations are from The New Revised Standard Version of the Bible, Anglicised edition, copyright © 1989, 1995 by the Division of Christian Education of the National Council of the churches of Christ in the United States of America. Used by permission. All rights reserved.

Scripture quotations on cover and title page are taken from The Holy Bible, New International Version (Anglicised edition) copyright © 1979, 1984, 2011 by Biblica. Used by permission of Hodder & Stoughton Publishers, a Hachette UK company. All rights reserved. 'NIV' is a registered trademark of Biblica. UK trademark number 1448790.

Photograph on page 52 copyright © Lightstock; photographs on pages 4, 11, 16, 19, 20, 26, 32, 38, 44 and 62 copyright © Tom Milton and the Birmingham Methodist Circuit.

Every effort has been made to trace and contact copyright owners for material used in this resource. We apologise for any inadvertent omissions or errors, and would ask those concerned to contact us so that full acknowledgement can be made in the future.

A catalogue record for this book is available from the British Library

Printed and bound by CPI Group (UK) Ltd, Croydon CR0 4YY

CONTENTS

Introduction 6

UNDERSTANDING THE HABIT 9

  Worship resources 10

  Group material and activities 24

FORMING THE HABIT 35

  Stories to show the habit forming 36

  Practices to help form the habit 39

  Questions to consider as a church 46

  Connecting the habits 47

GOING FURTHER WITH THE HABIT 49

  Understanding the nature and purpose of the Bible 50

  Arts and media 55

To order more copies of the Holy Habits resources, or to find out how to download pages for printing or projection on screen, please visit brfonline.org.uk/holy-habits.

Remember the context

This Holy Habit is set in the context of ten Holy Habits, and the ongoing life of your church and community.

> **They devoted themselves to the apostles' teaching** and fellowship, to the breaking of bread and the prayers. Awe came upon everyone, because many wonders and signs were being done by the apostles. All who believed were together and had all things in common; they would sell their possessions and goods and distribute the proceeds to all, as any had need. Day by day, as they spent much time together in the temple, they broke bread at home and ate their food with glad and generous hearts, praising God and having the goodwill of all the people. And day by day the Lord added to their number those who were being saved.
>
> ACTS 2:42–47

A prayer for the faithful practice of Holy Habits

This prayer starts with a passage from Romans 5:4–5.

> Endurance produces character, and character produces hope,
>   and hope does not disappoint us…
> Gracious and ever-loving God, we offer our lives to you.
> Help us always to be open to your Spirit in our thoughts
>   and feelings and actions.
> Support us as we seek to learn more about those habits of the Christian life
>   which, as we practise them, will form in us the character of Jesus
>   by establishing us in the way of faith, hope and love.
> Amen

INTRODUCTION

Holy Habits is about practising doing holy things until they become instinctive. In this booklet, we explore the habit of the early Christians in which 'they devoted themselves to the apostles' teaching'.

The opening chapters of Acts present a continuum of ministry from Jesus through the apostles. Jesus had a teaching ministry which was rooted in the Hebrew scriptures (the Old Testament of the Christian Bible). This is continued through those who were first identified as his disciples – the apostles in Luke's narrative. James Dunn argues that:

> The apostles are the medium and the guarantors of the teaching focused on fresh interpretations of the scriptures and beginning to order the memories of Jesus' teaching and ministry into forms suitable for instruction, worship and proclamation.
>
> James D.G. Dunn, *The Acts of the Apostles* (Epworth, 1996), p. 35

So the teaching is **Biblical Teaching**, drawing on the Hebrew scriptures, out of which Jesus taught, and Jesus' own teaching, much of which went on to be recorded in the New Testament. For us, **Biblical Teaching** includes also the letters and Revelation, which were written after the events in Acts 2.

With this habit, it is particularly important to both explore it and live it. The four words 'they devoted themselves to' are important. In exploring this Holy Habit, it is hoped that you will not just discover more of what the Bible says, but renew your devotion to applying **Biblical Teaching** so as to grow in grace and holiness and thereby help to transform the world to reflect the kingdom values we discover in the scriptures.

We can explore **Biblical Teaching** on our own, and even better together. We need to engage imaginatively, critically, prayerfully and contextually. Your exploration of this Holy Habit can provide the opportunity to engage with **Biblical Teaching** in different ways and then to live out the insights you gain.

Reflections

We develop a Holy Habit of 'devoting ourselves to the apostles' teaching' by paying loving attention to the whole of the Bible, wrestling even with the parts we do not like or find difficult. We listen, read, reflect and respond. We pray and put it into action. We deliberately practise doing all that until it becomes completely instinctive.

This habit is called **Biblical Teaching**, but that does not mean that that there is only one way to understand a particular passage, or to apply it to our lives. In the Gospels, Jesus makes points and states morals. However, he also speaks enigmatically or in parables, telling stories that go beyond making a particular point; they stimulate our imaginations, confound our expectations and lead us to see in new ways God's love and grace working in the world and in our lives.

Biblical scholarship is helpful, but the Holy Habit starts with ordinary people who tell their story and look to connect it with the stories in the Bible; or who read the Bible and look to connect it with their own experience. When practised together, the Holy Habit of **Biblical Teaching** is perhaps best described as 'the people of God, gathering around the word of God, sharing their insights into the gospel in order to discover the Holy Spirit's insights among the people'. So we move from reading or listening to passages of the Bible to hearing God speaking to us in and through them.

As you discover more of what the Bible says and how it can guide your living, we pray that you will develop a passion for **Biblical Teaching** that will change your life, and the world through you.

 Resources particularly suitable for children and families

 Resources particularly suitable for young people

CH4   Church Hymnary 4 (also known as Hymns of Glory Songs of Praise)
RS   Rejoice and Sing
SoF   Songs of Fellowship 6
StF   Singing the Faith

Different ways in which Christians understand how the Bible speaks to us

Later in this booklet you are invited to reflect imaginatively on the account in Luke 24:13–50 of how Jesus appears to two disciples. They are walking from Jerusalem to Emmaus after Jesus' resurrection, not knowing quite what to believe. In this passage, we see Jesus referring to 'the scriptures' to explain his suffering to these disciples.

The passage doesn't tell us how Jesus used the books of Moses and the writings of the prophets to explain the events of the past few days to the two disciples. So, did Jesus point to verses that would prove particular points – using scripture to provide proof? In fact, he couldn't have done that in a way which a modern Christian might imagine, because there weren't any divisions into numbered verses and chapters in the original Hebrew version, as there are in our translations. If we turn to other parts of the New Testament, we get a sense of how Jesus might have used the Hebrew scriptures on this occasion.

In the sermon on the mount, Jesus refers to statements in the Old Testament: 'You have heard that it was said… but I say to you…' (see Matthew 5:21–48). Jesus takes his stand within the biblical revelation, but he is not restricted by it. That principle of freedom from the 'letter of the law' is spelled out explicitly by Paul in 2 Corinthians 3:1–17. You may wish to read what Paul says there and reflect on it as you engage with the rest of this booklet.

Later on, you can read more about how two different denominations affirm the biblical basis of their faith and life, following the teaching of Jesus. Each of these churches had to think through their understanding of the authority of the Bible very thoroughly and clearly, in the process of producing statements about the nature and role of scripture which would help bring previously separated churches into united churches. You may wish to jump ahead at this stage in order to help clarify your own thinking before proceeding with your study of **Biblical Teaching**. But, whenever you do this, it is very important that you approach the rest of **Biblical Teaching** with an awareness of the different ways in which Christians understand how the Bible speaks to us. How do we use the Bible as Jesus used it on the road to Emmaus? Is it merely the record of what people experienced and thought about God thousands of years ago? Is it a divinely given textbook which we can refer to in order to get concise instructions on how to deal with anything and everything in life? What is the role of the Holy Spirit, and of the body of Christ of which we are part, in our reading, interpretation and application of scripture? These are the kinds of questions with which we must get to grips if we are to approach **Biblical Teaching** with the God-given discernment which the Bible itself urges on us (see, for example, 2 Timothy 3:16–17 or Hebrews 5:11–14).

UNDERSTANDING THE HABIT

WORSHIP RESOURCES

Below are some thoughts and ideas for how you might incorporate this Holy Habit into worship.

Biblical material

Old Testament passages:

- Genesis 1:1—2:3   Creation
- Exodus 24:1–8   God speaks to and through Moses
- Deuteronomy 17:14–20   Ruling by constant reference to the scriptures
- Psalm 119   Walking in the law of the Lord
- Isaiah 55:1–11   God's word will accomplish God's purposes
- Ezekiel 3:1–11   Nurtured by God's word to speak God's words

Gospel passages:

- Matthew 22:34–40   Jesus summarises God's commandments
- Luke 4:1–13   Jesus resists temptation three times by reference to scripture
- Luke 4:14–30   Jesus reads, preaches and fulfils scripture
- Luke 24:13–50   The road to Emmaus
- John 1:1–18   The Word becomes flesh

Other New Testament passages:

- Acts 2:14–41; 3:12–26   Peter preaches
- Acts 8:26–40   Philip and the Ethiopian
- Romans 15:1–6   Through the scriptures we have hope
- Colossians 3:12–17   Let the word of the Lord dwell in you richly
- 2 Timothy 3:14—4:5   Faith in Christ enables us to interpret the scriptures

Suggested hymns and songs

- Break thou the bread of life (RS 314, StF 153)
- Come, divine Interpreter (StF 154)
- Come, Holy Ghost, our hearts inspire (StF 155)
- Come, living God, when least expected (CH4 609, RS 354)
- God has spoken – by his prophets (StF 157)
- Help us, O Lord, to learn (StF 501)
- Jesus is Lord! Creation's voice proclaims it (RS 268, StF 353)
- Jesus the Lord said: 'I am the Bread' (RS 199, StF 252)
- Lord, thy word abideth (RS 317)
- Master, speak! Thy servant heareth (StF 666)
- Not far beyond the sea nor high (RS 318, StF 159)
- Now in reverence and awe (SoF 1468)
- Powerful in making us wise to salvation (StF 160)
- Prepare our hearts, O God (SoF 3031)
- Speak, O Lord (StF 161)
- Thanks to God whose word was spoken (CH4 605, RS 319)
- The prophets' voice comes down the years (StF 162)
- The Spirit of the Lord revealed (RS 311)
- Thy word (SoF 1066)
- We have a gospel to proclaim (CH4 363, StF 418)
- You're the word of God the Father (SoF 1669)
- Your hand, O God, has guided (CH4 511, RS 567, StF 692)
- Your words to me are life and health (RS 321, StF 164)

Introduction to the theme 👪

For this Holy Habit, two introductions to the theme are suggested. These could be used in two consecutive services, or at different points during a single service.

The importance of biblical teaching – Colossians 3:12–17

Have a selection of dressing-up clothes and invite volunteers to come and try something on. If people are willing, invite them to walk up and down the catwalk (aisle). Play some music to accompany them.

Talk together about what clothes are needed for different occasions or activities (e.g. work, sport, going out).

Talk about how Paul calls the Colossians to clothe themselves with garments of holiness – compassion, kindness, humility, meekness, patience, love, peace and thankfulness (Colossians 3:12–17). Invite the congregation to talk about what that might look like.

Remind them that developing, nurturing and embedding the Holy Habits will clothe us in the garments of holiness.

See how many of the Holy Habits the congregation can recall. Can anyone recall from memory Acts 2:42–47?

Talk to the congregation about the Holy Habit of **Biblical Teaching** and what that means. (You may find it helpful to refer to the Introduction.)

Read Colossians 3:16–17 and break it into three parts:

- Explain how letting 'the word of Christ dwell in you richly' is achieved by studying and living God's word.
- Talk about the importance of learning from God's word together: 'teach and admonish one another in all wisdom'.
- Think about different ways of learning from God's word, through music, dance, drama and art: 'with gratitude in your hearts sing psalms, hymns, and spiritual songs to God'.

To close, pray the Holy Habits prayer (see p. 5), or you could sing 'With psalms and hymns and spiritual songs' by Steve Morgan-Gurr.

Exploring the books of the Bible – the whole Bible

How well does your Christian community know its Bible? We are in a generation now where many who come to faith will not have a traditional Sunday school grounding. This is a fun way to introduce the idea of the Bible as a 'library' rather than one homogenous book. It can be adapted in many ways for different contexts.

Prepare 66 strips of coloured paper – representing the spines of books on the shelf – and write or print on each one the name of one book of the Bible. Each category of book (poetry, history, wisdom, etc.) should be on a different colour. Either hide the 'books' around the worship/meeting space in advance, or give them out to people as they arrive.

You may wish to bring in a range of different books to show people and let them choose one each or one per small group to have a look at, e.g. cookery book, knitting patterns, car manual, DIY instructions, storybook/novel, poetry, hymn book, art book, history book, textbook, atlas, diary.

Go round and ask:

- What kind of book do you have?
- What is it for?
- Who is it for?
- Who wrote it?

Explain that the Bible (literal meaning: 'library') is a collection of lots of different types of writing that help us in different ways. In this activity, we are going to form the Bible library.

Invite people to search for the hidden strips or begin to collect those given out as people arrived. As the 'books' are found or collected, the aim is to build up your library and eventually to make a Bible with all 66 books in place – so you will need to keep moving fairly fast. People can put the books of the same colour together, or decide as they go along where they will go in the 'library'. As the groups build, invite people to observe what those of the same colour have in common. If there is sufficient knowledge (or using a Bible), organise the books into Bible order.

During the collation, you can share the following information about the Bible. You might want to reflect on this again at the end of the exercise.

- We usually meet the Bible bound as one book, but it was written by many different authors over a period of years.
- In some cases, we are confident about who wrote the individual books, in other cases we are less certain.
- In this one book, we find anthologies, stories, history and law (if all ages are present, you may need to use other terms). A good way to think of this is to imagine the shelves in a library. If we wanted to read about someone's life, we might turn to biographies; for a more personal insight, we might find some of their letters; to understand what is accepted, we might need to look up the legal situation under 'law'.
- In a library, information is not stored in the order it was written in and the Bible is the same.

Once all the strips have come forward and are laid in place, invite people to share their reflections on the exercise. Does it help knowing that there are different types of books and writing in the Bible, written by different people at different times? What questions does this raise for you?

Conclude with a reflection or conversation about the rich resources we have in the Bible and about how we continue to learn from it and be inspired by it and are challenged to interpret what it means for our living today.

Round off in prayer, giving thanks for those who wrote the books we have in the Bible and for those who help us to understand them. Pray too for the help of the Holy Spirit to both understand and live out the teachings of the Bible in everyday life and action.

Colossians 3:12–17

Paul's letter to the Colossians is an excellent place in which to explore the importance of devotion to **Biblical Teaching**. One of Paul's motives for writing the letter was to address what is sometimes called 'the Colossian heresy'. This appears to have centred on a view that faith in Christ was not sufficient for salvation and that a variety of mystical experiences and (mainly Jewish) ritual practices were also needed. Colossians reminds us of the need to reflect on what the Bible does and doesn't say and to be careful that we don't lay burdens on others or create value systems that have no foundation in scripture, however attractive or popular they may sound e.g. 'Charity starts at home'.

In this particular passage, Paul opens with a call to the Colossians to clothe themselves with garments of holiness: compassion, kindness, humility, meekness, patience, love, peace and thankfulness. As you explore Holy Habits, it is important to remember that they are *holy* habits. You may wish to pause and reflect on your journey thus far. How are the habits you have explored forming holiness in you individually and as a church?

If you are looking for a text to build a sermon upon about **Biblical Teaching**, then verse 16 is particularly appropriate:

> Let the word of Christ dwell in you richly; teach and admonish one another in all wisdom; and with gratitude in your hearts sing psalms, hymns, and spiritual songs to God.

You could explore this in two parts. First, reflect upon the opening words, 'Let the word of Christ dwell in you richly'. In some Greek manuscripts, the text reads 'let the word of God dwell in you'. The Greek used for 'word' is *logos* – which is most famously found in the prologue to John's Gospel. You may wish to explore the richness of this word and concept in the context of thinking about **Biblical Teaching**. How do understandings of the written word, the spoken word and the living word impact on our engagement with and, critically, our living of **Biblical Teaching**? As ever, Paul is keen to see **Biblical Teaching** lived out and, towards the end of the letter, he speaks of how the word of Christ might be lived out in the family (3:18–21), at work (3:22–4:1), in the church (4:2–4) and in life in general (4:5–6). Please note that these verses are not all straightforward and illustrate why we need to handle **Biblical Teaching** with care.

You may also wish to reflect on Paul's encouragement to 'dwell' in the word of Christ. Again, this is a very important phrase when it comes to Holy Habits. If the habits are to be fully formative and transformative, we need to dwell in them. For ideas on how we might dwell in **Biblical Teaching**, see the ideas for 'Forming the habit' later on.

The second part of verse 16 that you may wish to work on is Paul's instruction to 'teach and admonish one another in all wisdom; and with gratitude in your hearts sing psalms, hymns, and spiritual songs to God'. The phrase 'one another' is interesting. Australian New Testament lecturer Sylvia Wilkey-Collinson has studied the rabbinical teaching methods of Jesus in depth. Drawing on that study and her knowledge of good adult teaching practices, she advocates a 'Discipling Model of Teaching' for the fruitful nurture of disciples today. Her model has six key characteristics. It is:

1 relational
2 intentional (all members have a responsibility for learning)
3 mainly informal and life related
4 typically communal
5 reciprocal (learning is mutual and collaborative)
6 centrifugal in focus (disciples go out from the community to be involved in service and mission and then return to reflect).

While not disputing the view that some are graced with a particular gift of teaching, she strongly affirms the view that teaching and learning are gifts of the whole community:

> Although some may have a gift of teaching which they frequently use… all members of the community have a responsibility for enriching and contributing to the up-building of others. This is achieved in part by the exercise of their spiritual gifts and the example of their faithful, Christ-like living. Learning thus becomes a mutual, collaborative affair.
>
> Sylvia Wilkey-Collinson, *Making Disciples* (Paternoster, 2004), p. 241

You may wish to explore this and consider how more people may participate in the teaching offered by your church.

Finally, you could also think how 'psalms, hymns, and spiritual songs' and not just sermons, talks and studies might help people engage with and live out **Biblical Teaching**.

Prayers

Dear Father God,

We ask that you will help us to learn more about you through the Bible.

May you guide us through life
with the knowledge and understanding from your teachings
as we learn about you from Jesus' parables.

Please help us to grow closer to you
by focusing on your ways as Jesus taught.
Amen

Prayers from the Bible

The Bible includes many prayers that can be used today in worship, for example many of the psalms, the Magnificat (Luke 1:46–55), the Benedictus (Luke 1:68–79) and the Nunc dimittis (Luke 2:29–32).

A prayer for inspiration

The collect for Bible Sunday in *The Methodist Worship Book*, p. 561.

Blessed Lord,
who caused all holy scripture to be written for our learning:
help us so to hear them,
read, mark and inwardly digest them,
that through patience and the comfort of your holy word
we may embrace and ever hold fast
the hope of everlasting life
which you have given us.
In our saviour, Jesus Christ
Amen

Prayers from young people 👪 ☺

The following prayers were written by young people and children around the theme of **Biblical Teaching**. Use them as they are or as the inspiration to encourage your children and young people to write their own prayers for your services.

Dear Lord,
We thank you for all you have done for us,
for teaching us now
and when you first gave your word to the people.
May you teach us now and evermore.
Amen

Dear Lord.
We thank you for everything you do for us.
Thank you for teaching us your ways through your Word, the Bible.
Thank you, God, for showing us your love by sending us your son to die for us.
Thank you for showing us your forgiveness through the story of the prodigal son.
Thank you for showing us your greatness through the stories of creation.
Thank you for wanting us to be with you by showing us the way and guiding us.
Amen

Dear God,
Our world which you have provided is imperfect –
your kindness being ignored,
your creatures being persecuted.
As a community we are sorry for our many blemishes;
as a church, we are sorry we ignore your Bible,
which is so wise and so easy to forget.
Though we will probably be bad citizens again,
we ask for your forgiveness and admit our sins.
Sorry.
Amen

Dear God,
We're sorry for the times we don't follow your ways
as recorded in your word, the Bible.
We're sorry for the times when we don't follow the teachings of Jesus
and instead choose to neglect your ways.
Please forgive us for our sins
and let us try again to live as your son Jesus taught us.
Amen

Dear God,
In the Bible we read about wars and people seeking refuge.
We are worried about the wars and conflicts around the world.
Please let the wars stop and help refugees find a safe place to live.
Please help us make it a more peaceful place for the citizens in the country.
Help the families in war-torn areas live their lives in peace.
Amen

Dearest Father,
Please help us to understand your Bible and your Fellowship.
May you give us wisdom in our daily tasks and help us through life.
Amen

A prayer of gathering

Invite the congregation to reflect on the following words. Follow this with a period of silent reflection.

We gather to read, to listen,
yearning for your yes,
hoping to hear
the one word of truth
that might settle our doubts,
quieten our questioning,
nail down meaning,
once for all.

But you came to us crosswise,
questioning our questions,
whispering on the edge of hearing
something that calls to us:
snatches of a conversation
old as the world,
still unfinished.

Different ways of praying

A listening prayer

After the sermon or Bible readings, ask the congregation to sit in silence, with eyes open or closed, hands held open in their laps.

Invite them to listen to what God is saying to them.

You could play an appropriate piece of music.

A wondering prayer

God is creator of our creativity and our imagination. Invite the congregation to wonder about the passage you are exploring together. You will need to adapt the sentences to fit the passage. You could 'wonder' your way through the whole passage using the words and phrases in the text.

Inform people that after each phrase there will be plenty of silence to allow them to let God work with their imaginations.

At the end, take time to allow people to share where their wondering has taken them.

God, creator of our creativity and our imagination
I wonder what it would have been like to have been there
    that day/in that place…
I wonder what it would have been like to have witnessed…
I wonder how [Name] felt when…
I wonder what s/he could see…
I wonder how [Name] was changed by what happened…
I wonder how I would have reacted had I been there…
I wonder how it made you feel…
I wonder what you want me to learn from this passage…
I wonder how it relates to my life/the life of this church/this community…
God of wonder, help me to see all things with your eyes
and understand all things with your mind.
Amen

Praying the Bible

Choose a psalm or Bible passage and pray the text slowly.

Repeat lines or the whole passage, or hold long periods of silence between the verses or lines.

A prayer of confession

Ask the congregation to think about how they have failed to follow God's word and done things they regret. Invite them to write these down on small pieces of paper, in words, symbols or initials as they feel most comfortable.

Explain that you are going to read a psalm and encourage them, as the verses are read, to offer what they have written to God and to ask forgiveness.

Read Psalm 32, 38 or 51 (or selected verses).

As the words of pardon are read, encourage them to rip up the paper and place the pieces in a metal bin at the front of the church.

If it is safe to do so, burn or shred the paper as a sign of God's forgiveness. Dispose of any remnants safely and securely.

Acrostic prayers

A number of the Psalms in the Bible are acrostic psalms, where each line starts with the next letter of the alphabet. Try writing your own acrostic psalm as a prayer.

Start the first line of your psalm with the letter A, start the next with a B, and then carry on using the next letter of the alphabet to begin each new line (you might not get through the whole alphabet!).

You may find it helpful to give people a topic to write their psalm about, or to specifically focus on praise, or you may prefer to encourage people to write about whatever is on their hearts and minds.

GROUP MATERIAL AND ACTIVITIES

Some of these small group materials are traditional Bible studies, some are more diverse session plans and others are short activities, reflections and discussions. Please choose materials appropriate to whatever group you are working with.

Learning together in community

Acts 8:26–40

It is easy to think that Bible studies should only be led by someone with academic training in theology, but while they might have particular gifts and insights to offer, all those who gather around the Bible have a part to play in opening up its teaching. We all bring our own experiences of life, and our own questions about what the text means for us. A group from the Birmingham Methodist Circuit with no academic theological training, just a passion for the Bible, prepared the original version of this study, both to share their insights and to encourage other groups to do likewise.

Spend a few moments either as a group or individually thinking about how and when you read the Bible, what you find most helpful and why. What helps you to live out the Holy Habits?

Read Acts 8:26–40.

The story focuses on two characters: Philip and the Ethiopian official. Who are they? What do you make of them? Look at what is said about each character and note what they have in common and how they differ. This is not a natural teacher-and-student relationship. How would each character have felt talking with the other one?

In verse 27, we hear that the Ethiopian is returning from worship yet later, in verse 31, he declares that he does not understand the scripture he is reading. 'How can I, unless someone guides me?' (Acts 8:31).

- Do you always understand what is written in the Bible? What would help?
- If you find something that you don't understand, what do you do? Where do you take your questions?

Verse 31 says that the Ethiopian invited Philip to join him in the carriage. The Ethiopian took a risk, but so did Philip. Through taking the risk they both gained much.

- Who would you expect to teach you about the Bible?
- Do you ever consider your own interpretation less valid than others?
- Has there been a time when someone who you would not expect to teach you opened your eyes to what a Bible passage meant?
- Do we invite people into our churches, youth or home groups and expect to learn from them?

There are many different ways to read the Bible. God can speak to anyone through the Bible and therefore we can all learn from one another irrespective of our education, age or experience. Different groups may read the Bible in different ways: young or old, black or white, male or female. Why not encourage someone who comes from a different perspective to explain what specific passages mean to them and how those passages shape their living?

The Ethiopian hears Philip's interpretation and immediately feels compelled to be baptised himself.

- Has a passage in the Bible, or a new understanding of a biblical passage, ever touched you and made you respond in a way that you would never have expected to respond?

The Holy Spirit led Philip and gave him the courage to take a risk.

- When has the Holy Spirit guided us, or given us courage?
- Have we felt the Spirit's presence in a special way when reading the Bible?
- How does the Holy Spirit help us to live out **Biblical Teaching**?

The road to Emmaus

Luke 24:13–50

This reflective exercise on a biblical passage could be used in a small group or as a meditation in a service of **Worship**. It involves inviting people to place themselves into the text and imagine their responses to the events in the narrative. The meditation makes connections between **Biblical Teaching** and several of the other Holy Habits.

Read the piece out slowly, pausing for a good amount of time as you go to allow people to dwell in the word and to let the scriptures and the Spirit speak to them. The verse numbers are there for reference and don't need to be read out.

You and one of the other disciples are getting out of Jerusalem. As you go, you are trying to make sense of what has happened (vv. 13–14).

Are you scared or just completely confused?

A stranger joins you as you go, but you do not recognise him. Why? Are you so wrapped up in what has happened, or is it because you are not expecting to see him, or is there another reason (vv. 15–16)?

The stranger joins in your conversation. Then he starts to refer to passages in the Hebrew scriptures which he says talk of a messiah suffering and then being glorified, and which he then implies refer to Jesus (although he is not yet saying directly that he is Jesus) (vv. 25–27).

To which scriptures is he referring? Irritatingly, Luke does not tell us in detail. Which passages do you think he may be referring to?

Jesus is reinterpreting and reapplying the scriptures to help you reinterpret your own experience, see more clearly what God is doing in it, and reapply yourself to your discipleship. You feel comforted and excited. It fires you up (v. 32). How do you respond?

You invite him in to the place where you are staying. You allow him to take over as the host. Then something about the way he takes bread, blesses it, breaks it and shares it with you reminds you of the last supper and all the other meals you shared with Jesus (vv. 28–30). All at once, you realise that this is Jesus (v. 31)! How do you feel now?

Breaking Bread and exploring the scriptures have enabled you to explore your experience and discover things in it that you were not recognising before. They have enabled you to welcome the risen Christ into your life. You cease to see him as you used to do, because he is living within you (v. 32).

This turns you round. Rather than running away, you go back to re-engage with the other disciples. You listen to their experience. You discover that since you left, Peter has not just seen the tomb is empty but has met the risen Lord! You then share your experience and your new understanding with them (vv. 33–35).

What does this say about the place and value of another Holy Habit, **Fellowship**?

Suddenly you all experience Jesus present among you. You realise that this is not a ghost or some new spiritual being. It is the Jesus you knew before he was crucified, but now alive in a new way (vv. 36–43).

He again explores the scriptures with you. That helps you understand what is happening to you. Understanding your experience better helps you understand the scriptures better. Then, again, you cease to see him as you did before. You prepare to go out and bear witness to these things in all the world (vv. 44–50). Soon you will feel yourself strangely warmed – this time, not just in your heart. You will find yourself fired up by the Spirit to be the body of Christ in the world (Acts 2).

How do you respond to this in **Worship**? How do you respond to this in **Prayer**?

What do you imagine that you are going to do by way of **Serving** or encouraging others to follow afresh the Jesus you have encountered?

Might you explore other biblical passages this way?

Bible as guide? 👪 ☺

The whole Bible

When the Church of England broke away from the church of Rome in the 16th century, one of the key issues was the authority of the Bible. The English Reformers' understanding of biblical authority was encapsulated in Article 6 of the Thirty-nine Articles of faith which they drew up:

> Holy scripture containeth all things necessary to salvation: so that whatsoever is not read therein, nor may be proved thereby, is not to be required of any man, that it should be believed as an article of the Faith, or be thought requisite or necessary to salvation.

What does this statement say about the Bible as guide? What does it not say about the Bible as guide? At this point, if you haven't already read the piece on 'Understanding the nature and purpose of the Bible' (see p. 50), you may wish to do so in order to engage with the question of the balance between the Bible and the Holy Spirit as we seek God's guidance, in our lives and in the church. It is important that you think about this carefully before undertaking the following activity.

Activity and discussion
Create a maze/labyrinth or easy obstacle course and play in pairs. One person is blindfolded, and the other acts as a guide, either by calling instructions from the sidelines or by going ahead and leading their partner by the hand.

If you have or can borrow a floor labyrinth painted on a sheet, you could use this as your course. Or try using chairs, cardboard boxes, mats, etc. Prevent trip hazards!

Once everyone has had a turn, talk about their experiences. How did it feel to be unaware of the path ahead? To trust someone else? Was it easier to hear instructions or to follow a physical lead? Can they relate this experience to following Jesus?

Show the group some camping equipment such as a map, compass, torch or walking stick.

Discuss with people how each item helps on a journey. Explain that, for Christians, the Bible is seen as a guide on their journey through life. But add that this cannot be divorced from the leading and guidance of the Holy Spirit (see Romans 8:1–14, especially verse 14, in conjunction with 2 Timothy 3:14–17).

We need to take seriously this charge to Timothy:

> But as for you, continue in what you have learned and firmly believed, knowing from whom you learned it, and how from childhood you have known the sacred writings that are able to instruct you for salvation through faith in Christ Jesus. All scripture is inspired by God and is [or alternatively, Every scripture inspired by God is also] useful for teaching, for reproof, for correction, and for training in righteousness, so that everyone who belongs to God may be proficient, equipped for every good work.
>
> 2 Timothy 3:14–17

It is important to realise, though, that the sacred writings which Timothy knew from childhood were the Hebrew scriptures. Christians believe that the Old Testament points to 'salvation through faith in Christ' but this is something that is not at all obvious to most sincere Jewish readers, and for Christians it needs to be discerned through the guidance of the Holy Spirit.

Verses to look up:

- Psalm 119:11: 'I treasure your word in my heart, so that I may not sin against you.'
- Psalm 119:105: 'Your word is a lamp to my feet and a light to my path.'
- Hebrews 4:12: 'Indeed, the word of God is living and active, sharper than any two-edged sword, piercing until it divides soul from spirit, joints from marrow; it is able to judge the thoughts and intentions of the heart.'

Ask the group how the Holy Spirit guides, on the pathway of living out **Biblical Teaching**.

What is the word of God?
Look up John 1:1. How is the title 'the Word' applied in John's Gospel?

James Dunn tells us that, in Judaism before the time of Jesus, Jews came to use Wisdom, Word and Spirit all as terms that spoke of the active presence of God in the world (James D.G. Dunn, *Christology in the Making: A New Testament enquiry into the origins of the doctrine of the incarnation*, 2nd edition, Eerdmans, 1989). So to read these verses above about the word of God as referring simply to the Bible is not accurate. Christians believe, however, that the Bible is intimately connected with the active presence of God in the world. Get the group to discuss how this applies in their own understanding and experience.

Divide a large piece of paper into sections, including things such as family, friends, celebrities, teachers, youth leaders, parents, the internet, books, magazines, the Bible, etc.

Give each person some counters or tiddlywinks. Ask them the following questions and ask them to place their counters on the relevant section of paper to answer each question.

Who or what would you look to when making a decision about:

- what to wear?
- what hobby to do?
- how to treat a new person?
- what job you should do?
- how to learn a new skill?

- whether to forgive someone or not?
- a moral dilemma (you could think of some examples relevant to the age/context of the group)?

You may like to add more questions.

At the end of the exercise, discuss whether the group felt that they would look to the Bible for guidance, and why or why not.

Explain that many Christians look at what the Bible says alongside other things such as tradition, experience or their reason, to work out what guidance the Bible is offering.

You could take a simple example to explain this, such as guidance about what a person should eat. Look at what is literally said in the Bible about what you should eat, and then compare that with how Christians have – or have not – applied it literally. Draw out how complex it can be for Christians to hold all of these things in tension when making decisions, while recognising the authority of the Bible.

If you want to know a little more about how scripture, tradition, reason and experience might work together in a Christian view of authority, see the final paragraph of the section at the end of this booklet on 'How does a Christian read the Bible' (p. 53).

Bible in context 👪 ☺

It is important to understand the context of when the Bible was written. You could spend time researching with your group some of the authors of the Bible, when sections were written, etc.

To get a 'bigger picture' of the overarching story of the Bible, of God's love for his creation and outworking of salvation, you could look at a Bible timeline. Scripture Union has display versions and mini pocket size versions:

- For youth: **www.scriptureunion.org.uk/162233**
- For 5–11s: **www.scriptureunion.org.uk/162247**
- For under-5s: **www.scriptureunion.org.uk/68461**

The youth resource 'Navigate' (**www.methodist.org.uk/navigate**) has a session plan exploring the overarching story of the Bible, with a number of different activities and video clips (session 2 in particular).

Alternatively, you could spend time over a series of weeks making your own timeline. Don't forget, as you read different passages each week, to talk about what style of writing it is in, who may have written it and where it fits into the overall story.

I wonder 👪

'Godly Play' (**www.godlyplay.uk**) explores Bible stories using objects and symbols as well as words, in order to help those who share in the stories become more aware of God's presence in their lives. The focus is not on the storyteller, but on the storytelling materials and on the story.

In preparing for a session, the storyteller memorises a script and internalises the story, and reflects and works on it. The conversation that will take place in the group will then focus on the participants' responses.

In an 'I wonder' section, the thinking and feeling about the story comes from the participants, where they are in their lives at that moment, their concerns, worries and joys. There is no prescribed conclusion, but a space to interpret.

Godly Play then aims to create a safe space where ideas, opinions and gifts are deeply respected and a model community might be formed which demonstrates how Christians might live together in a way that is biblical.

Religious language is used – parable, sacred story, silence and liturgical action. A pattern is followed beginning with being greeted at the door or threshold by a 'doorkeeper', which prepares participants to enter the storytelling community or circle. This preparation – creating a place for stilling and silence – is crucial.

The word of God in the story is then presented using visual materials, and this is followed by open, wondering questions. In the conversation, all contributions are equally valued.

Participants then respond by choosing an activity from the range of craft and arts materials provided, or exploring other Godly Play stories and books, or simply enjoying a quiet space.

To close the session, the group is brought back together to eat, drink and chat before a blessing and sending back into the world.

The Parable of the Deep Well

The material for the 'Parable of the Deep Well' explores **Biblical Teaching**. It is taken from the rabbinical tradition (the Midrash Rabbah). For a full script, see Jerome W. Berryman, *The Complete Guide to Godly Play: 20 presentations for winter* (Church Publishing Inc., 2002, 2011).

You will need props in a box (sized in proportion to your setting):

- a cylinder to represent a deep well
- some cloth to represent the desert
- a bucket
- strands of gold thread.

Invite participants to sit around you in a horseshoe. Take the props out of the box (without explaining what they are). Tell the story – emphasising the well's clear, cold, refreshing water.

Point out that the water is so far down that it can't be seen clearly. It is impossible to drink it. Imagine the crowds who reach the well but walk past. One person stops and wonders, looks at the well and sees a rusty object that looks like a cup and some golden strands. Ask how this cup might make drinking possible.

As the story continues, begin tying the threads together and attach the longer thread to the bucket.

The person who stopped lowers the bucket into the well and gets a cup of water to drink. It is life-changing. They leave the bucket and the long string by the well so that the next person can taste the water too.

Pretend to take a drink yourself and offer others the opportunity to pretend as well.

Continue with some open questions, such as:

- What might the water from the well be?
- What might the deep well be?
- Why did the person stop and wonder?
- What do you wonder about?

FORMING THE HABIT

The ideas presented in this section are offered to help you establish or further practise **Biblical Teaching** as a regular habit personally, as a church and in engagement with your local community and the wider world. You may want to consider using the ideas in more than one of these contexts.

In developing **Biblical Teaching** as a regular habit, you may find some of the material in the 'Understanding the habit' section helpful too.

STORIES TO SHOW THE HABIT FORMING

How could you use these formative and transformative stories to inspire others? What stories of your own could you share?

In the 2016 series of the BBC show *The Apprentice*, the candidates were filmed on a day off. Different people were doing different things. One of them, Samuel Boateng, a car salesman from London, was shown reading a book – the Bible. In an interview with Premier Radio, Samuel explained how engaging with the Bible and being devoted to its teaching shaped the way in which he conducted himself on the programme and enabled him to cope with the process: 'If it wasn't for these things [reading the Bible and praying] that were instilled in me from childhood, I would have struggled massively through the process'.

It's fascinating how Samuel sees engaging with the Bible and praying very much as habits. It's noteworthy too that these were habits shaped in childhood.

In the interview, Samuel goes on to speak of how his favourite books are 1 and 2 Samuel, and how he is particularly inspired by David's pursuit of holiness.

You can see the interview in full at **player.premier.org.uk/media/t/1_ gwfywyma** or by searching the Premier Radio Player for 'Samuel Boateng'. You may wish to reflect on how devotion to **Biblical Teaching** shapes your relationships and your conduct in the workplace.

In Andrew Roberts' book *Holy Habits* (Malcolm Down Publishing, 2016), he shares the story of a fresh expression centred on **Biblical Teaching**:

At Zac's Place in Swansea (known locally as 'a church for ragamuffins'), there is a sign next to the entrance that is refreshingly different. It says, 'No drugs, no guns and no explosives'. Immediately, you get the sense that this is going to be a lively place. And then what do you find at the heart of the community? An open Bible, as Pastor Sean Stillman explains:

'Building disciples is an unbelievably messy process and I think it was messy for Jesus and it continues to be so for us. We unashamedly focus a lot of attention to studying the Bible together; we call it our Tribal Gathering. We attract all sorts, we do some good old-fashioned Bible study topped and tailed with a prayer' (*Expressions: Making a difference*, Fresh Expressions, 2011, chapter 28).

So at this innovative newly forming Christian community, we find the same devotion to **Biblical Teaching** that Luke highlights in the very first church in Acts. Is this a hallmark of your church?

In the Birmingham Methodist Circuit, a different way of engaging with **Biblical Teaching** to form a Holy Habit impacted on those doing the teaching as much as those being taught:

With the decline of Sunday Schools, we were concerned at the lack of exposure children have to the amazing world of Bible stories. Stumbling upon the 'Open the Book' project (**www.biblesociety.org.uk/get-involved/open-the-book**) was an answer to prayer. Here was an opportunity to share the stories with over 300 children on a regular basis. Across three local churches, a group of 'would-be storytellers' and actors was assembled. The material itself was inspiring and the children loved it, listening with rapt attention and eagerly helping out with the dramas. Interestingly, the adults taking part found the whole experience fulfilling, even faith-deepening.

Planning meetings give everyone a chance to offer ideas and are invariably great fun. Set designers, sound and lighting effects, costumes and special effects all combine to bring these amazing stories to life. There's always a queue of volunteer extras and a little group who always wait afterwards to find out what the next story will be. As you walk around the community, often a small child will stand in front of you and say, 'Aren't you one of the storytellers? I love Open the Book!'

At the beginning we were worried that our efforts might appear a bit amateurish, but one small boy was seen to nudge his neighbour on the way out of assembly and heard to say, 'It's better than the films, 'ent it?' Perhaps best of all, we heard from a 14-year-old at his confirmation that his faith had sprung from being involved in the Open the Book stories at his primary school.

The Great 50 Days is a traditional name for the period from Easter Day to Pentecost, but it is a season we have not always emphasised in modern church life. Fifty Christians in the north-east decided to mark the period:

> Each took one of the resurrection to Pentecost Bible passages and wrote a short reflection and prayer prompt. These were published as a devotional resource for individuals and groups to an amazing response. New groups met for discussion in diverse places, from churches to pubs. Individuals were touched by particular reflections as insights were shared. Stories were told and shared. This was the first such regional resource, but after such a positive response a new edition themed on 'Following Jesus' was planned for 2017 and a small group of people agreed to bring it together. Search for 'The Great 50 Days' on social media or the web to find out more.

Might you use this or develop your own resource to help you to live out **Biblical Teaching**?

PRACTICES TO HELP FORM THE HABIT

Here are some suggestions for how **Biblical Teaching** can be part of a rhythm or rule of life in our personal discipleship and in and through the **Fellowship** of our churches.

If we are to be faithful, regular readers of the Bible, we need to be aware of how we read the Bible. Earlier in this booklet we considered the Bible as a library of different kinds of books. That leads us on to considering different kinds of meanings which biblical texts may bear, and different ways in which we might need to read the Bible.

Different ways of reading the Bible

The Vision4Life programme of the United Reformed Church (**www.vision4life.org. uk**) looks at ways of reading different kinds of content in a newspaper as a way of getting to grips with different ways in which we may need to read the Bible. Reflect on this as a comparison with how the Bible may need to be read in different ways.

If you wish to follow this up with a more detailed account, refer to the article, 'How to Read the Bible', by the Revd Dr Ian Paul, editor of Grove Books (**www.readers. cofe.anglican.org/u_d_lib_res/r31.pdf**). This article is a little over two pages in length and goes on to offer a very helpful list for further reading on the topic. The first section of the article is titled 'One question – many answers' and offers this introduction to the question of how to read the Bible:

> The question 'How do you drive your car?' could elicit a range of responses. 'Every Sunday,' 'With my heart in my mouth,' and 'By unlocking the door and getting in' are three possible kinds of answer. There are likewise different ways to answer the question 'How do you read the Bible?'

You may also find the page on how to read the Bible on the New Living Translation website helpful for some of the practical advice which it provides (**www. newlivingtranslation.com/02biblestudy/howtoread.asp**).

The page on how to read the Bible on a Catholic website, Presentation Ministries (**www.presentationministries.com/publications/HowToRead.asp**), is significant in the way it points us to the work of the Holy Spirit as the vital element in reading scripture 'in spirit and in truth'.

The *Bible Month* magazine offers four different ways of reading the Bible which are useful in small groups:

- *lectio divina*
- inductive Bible study – the Swedish method
- engaging with art
- inductive Bible study – the '5W' approach.

You can find out more in the first edition of *Bible Month*, on James, available at **www.methodist.org.uk/prayer-and-worship/bible-month**. Look for the four pages headed 'Small Group Resource', and note also that at least some of these might be good for individual reading of the Bible also.

Then, if you are in the market for something really meaty on the topic, you could read C.H. Spurgeon's sermon 'Reading the Bible' (**www.spurgeon.org/sermons/1503. php**) or Bishop Kallistos Ware's page, from an Eastern Orthodox perspective, on 'How to read your Bible' (**www.antiochian.org/content/how-read-your-bible**).

> ## Journalling
>
> Journalling is regularly reflecting on your experiences, thoughts and encounters with God and keeping a note of your reflections. See the Holy Habits Introductory Guide for more information.
>
> As you try to develop the habit of **Biblical Teaching**, note in your journal all the different ways you engage with the Bible. Reflect upon which you have found most helpful and a more positive experience. Reflect upon whether the way you read/listen to the Bible has changed. When have you noticed **Biblical Teaching** changing your actions, behaviours and thoughts? How has God challenged you? Have you noticed habits forming?

Read the Bible

The Bible is full of challenges and surprises! It can be helpful to begin by asking what surprises you in the piece you are reading. What does it make you want to know about it? What does it make you want to do? How does it connect with your own experience and with the world in which we live?

Daily reading of, and reflection upon, **Biblical Teaching** has long been a Christian habit. There are a myriad of ways in which this can be done, from traditional daily Bible notes to a burgeoning range of websites and apps. Maybe exploring this habit will prompt you to renew a pattern of daily reading or explore a different way of reflecting on **Biblical Teaching** on a daily basis. As a church, you may wish to invest in some resources to encourage people to start or renew this practice.

There are a wide range of resources available to help you form a habit of daily Bible reading, such as:

- BRF's range of Bible reading notes (**www.brf.org.uk/bible-reading**), including *New Daylight*, *Guidelines*, *Day by Day with God* and *The Upper Room*
- Scripture Union's E100 (100 'essential' Bible readings to give an overview of the Bible: **e100.scriptureunion.org.uk**) and WordLive (**www.wordlive.org**)
- Soul Survivor's 'Bible in a Year' (**bible.soulsurvivor.com**) – includes short videos about each day's reading
- HTB's 'Bible in One Year' (**www.bibleinoneyear.org**)
- UCB's Word for Today (**www.ucb.co.uk/word-for-today.html**)

Many of these are also available as apps for your smartphone or tablet. Note that they cover a range of theological perspectives and traditions and many others are available – why not explore a variety, including some from a tradition or perspective outside of your own?

For an in-depth exploration of the whole Bible, try Tom Wright's *For Everyone* commentary library. The whole resource runs to 18 volumes, so you may wish to see whether they are available to borrow from a library or local church.

Some Jewish people have mainlined the custom of wearing a phylactery, a small leather box containing the law of the Hebrew scriptures to remind them of their duty or calling to live by the teaching of those scriptures. Might you consider a Christian equivalent, such as wearing a wristband with a biblical verse or carrying a card in your wallet or purse with a verse of scripture (cards could be changed on a regular basis)?

Consider how you might get into habits of reading the Bible, or exploring Bible stories together as a family. There are a number of websites with resources for this, such as those offered by BRF (see **www.brf.org.uk/childrens-and-family-ministry**).

Between Advent 2008 and Advent 2011, United Reformed churches shared in the Vision4Life process. Materials were developed which sought to re-engage people with the Bible, prayer and evangelism and to transform the life of the local church. The extensive resources that were produced are available on the Vision4Life website (**www.vision4life.org.uk**).

Read the Bible

Gathering weekly, fortnightly or monthly to study the Bible in community also has a long and often fruitful history. If you already meet in such a way, how might you refresh this practice? If you don't, is this something you could introduce or reintroduce?

The big challenge with **Biblical Teaching** is how to live it. It is not always easy in a world of differing values. You might find a partner with whom you could regularly review:

- how **Biblical Teaching** has inspired you
- in what situations you have found it difficult to live out **Biblical Teaching**.

Connecting this with **Prayer** is very important.

As an extension to this, you may wish in your groups to use Jacqueline Jones' hymn 'Have you heard God's voice' and review events in the news against **Biblical Teaching**.

- Where in the news do you see **Biblical Teaching** being lived out?
- Where do you see it being challenged?
- Where might **Biblical Teaching** speak prophetically to situations in the news? How might you articulate this?

As a church, why not have a preaching or study series on one book of the Bible?

Hold each other accountable

Meet regularly with a small group of people (such as a house group, prayer triplet) and discuss how you are living out your faith. Hold each other accountable, so that the Bible is not just being read but is being lived.

It may be hard to do this at first if you are unused to it. You may find it helpful to start with some questions which are put to everyone, for instance:

- How is your relationship with God this week?
- How have you been challenged by God or the Bible this week?

The aim is not to criticise or condemn people, but to encourage people to be honest about how they are living their lives and, as they are held in mutual accountability, to find encouragement and support from others.

One group in Birmingham considered together how they were living out the Holy Habits. Some of the group helped someone move house (**Serving**). They go for coffee and cake (**Eating Together**), invite their friends (**Fellowship**), and have gathered together and acted as the worship band for two weddings between couples in the group (**Worship, Service, Sharing Resources** and **Fellowship**). These activities will be different in every group. What this group does show is the value of not just gathering together to study, but more importantly being proactive in getting together to be outward-focused too, in order to put what we read into practice together.

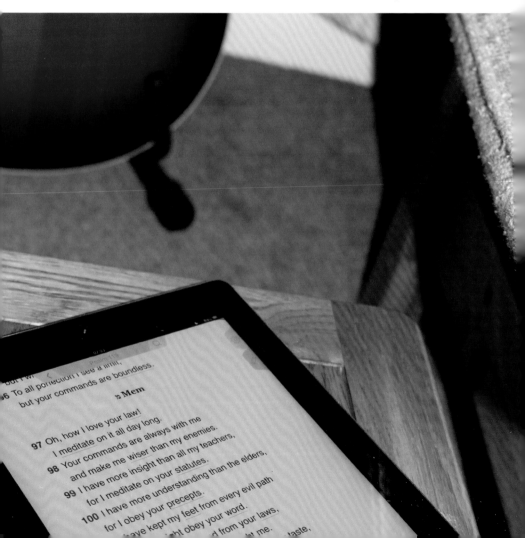

Read the Bible

Refresh your pattern of daily engagement with scripture or your regular Bible study group by trying a different approach using a different technique. Read the Bible, or hear it being read, in a different culture or context. Read the Bible with people of different ages (including children), ethnicities or languages. How do these differences change your perspective? Explore different ways of engaging with the Bible – reading different translations, or other interpretations (such as THE MESSAGE or The Street Bible), or approaching the Bible through artwork or other media.

Read the Bible in a different context or culture. How does the change of context affect the way in which **Biblical Teaching** speaks to you and shapes your living?

For young people, there are some examples of different ways to read the Bible in the 'Navigate' resources (**www.methodist.org.uk/navigate**).

Stretch yourself by reading an in-depth commentary on a book of the Bible.

Shake up your small group Bible study by doing a small group 'swap' – each group plans a Bible study for the other small group.

Do a course on the Bible individually or as a group. The *Disciple* course (**www.cokesbury.com/disciple**), for example, is a comprehensive way of exploring **Biblical Teaching**.

Interview some people in a service about the joys and struggles they have in living out **Biblical Teaching**.

Individually or as a church, practise a little **Gladness and Generosity** by funding the provision of Bibles for others or the work of Bible translators.

QUESTIONS TO CONSIDER AS A CHURCH

These questions will help your church to consider how it can review the place of **Biblical Teaching** in all of its life together. They are intended to be asked regularly rather than considered once and then forgotten. You will need to determine where in your church the responsibility for each question lies – with the whole church in a general meeting, or with the church leadership, a relevant committee or another grouping. Feel free to add more of your own.

- How does the life of your church show that you are living out devotion to **Biblical Teaching**? Explore specific examples.
- How does the life of your church show you are not living out devotion to **Biblical Teaching**? Explore specific examples.
- Are there aspects of **Biblical Teaching** that you neglect? What passages do you struggle with and how could you engage with them?
- What challenges to devotion to **Biblical Teaching** do members of your **Fellowship** face in day-to-day life? How might you support one another in the light of these challenges?
- How can you encourage and resource more biblical study and reflection in your life together, and in the lives of those who are part of the church? Do you need to form some new groups or refresh existing ones?
- Where does your congregation see **Biblical Teaching** at work in your community?
- In what ways does your congregation see **Biblical Teaching** contradicted in your community? How might you challenge that?
- When exploring the Bible in small groups or in services, who should be doing the teaching and who the learning? What contributions can children and young people offer?
- Do you need to review the practices of **Biblical Teaching** in your services of **Worship**?
- Reflect on the biblical names of God and how God is addressed in prayer: how is your praying affected by **Biblical Teaching**?
- How might you helpfully introduce people to biblical scholarship?
- What do you (or your congregation) consider to be the overarching message of the Bible? Is it possible to use this to unite (or explain) some seemingly disparate and sometimes contradictory positions in the Bible? Try doing this with different interpretations of the overarching message and see whether this reinforces or shatters some of your conceptions and/or preconceptions about the Bible.

CONNECTING THE HABITS

WORSHIP

Biblical Teaching can be presented and heard in a variety of ways in Worship, such as drama, art, hymns.

EATING TOGETHER

A shared meal is a great space in which to read and reflect on scripture, particularly for those seeking faith.

BREAKING BREAD

A balanced discipleship diet contains both word and sacrament (see the Emmaus road story). How might you develop this balance further?

MAKING MORE DISCIPLES

The gift of a Bible or a Gospel can be faith forming and life changing.

BIBLICAL TEACHING IS OUTWORKED IN ALL OF THE HOLY HABITS

The scriptures provide a rich trove of resources to inspire and aid Prayer.

PRAYER

SHARING RESOURCES

The Old Testament prophets in particular consistently call for a just, fair and generous society. You might wish to study some of them to better inform your Serving and Sharing Resources with Gladness and Generosity.

Biblical study has long been a centrepiece of Christian Fellowship. How might you refresh this tradition in different ways?

FELLOWSHIP

GLADNESS AND GENEROSITY

SERVING

GOING FURTHER WITH THE HABIT

UNDERSTANDING THE NATURE AND PURPOSE OF THE BIBLE

Different views on the Bible

The introduction to this habit at the start of this booklet explains how the teaching ministry of Jesus was rooted in the Old Testament scriptures, and how this was continued in the teaching of the apostles, so that in this booklet we focus on **Biblical Teaching**. At this point, we have to frankly acknowledge that there are major differences in the way that the nature of the Bible and of **Biblical Teaching** is understood. Two positions which would be on opposite ends of a spectrum of understanding the nature of the Bible might be characterised as follows:

- One position, close to the Muslim view of the Qu'ran, would be that the words of scripture were composed perfectly by God in heaven and were dictated to human agents to be written down as scripture.
- Another position, which might be held by non-Christians who have a sympathetic view of the Bible, is that it is 'inspired' in the same way that the work of Shakespeare may be regarded as inspired.

These two positions may not represent the views of any actual Christians, but they do illustrate the possibility of a range of different views on the Bible. A report to the 1998 Conference of the Methodist Church, 'A Lamp to My Feet and a Light to My Path', identified seven different 'models of biblical authority' held by people within the Methodist Church. (See **www.methodist.org.uk/downloads/conf-a-lamp-to-my-feet-1998.pdf**, pp. 36–39.) It is important to note that the report does not endorse any one of these perspectives as *the* official position, and people in other churches might hold still other positions, but you may be interested to consider where your own perspective might fit within this kind of range of views.

This raises the question of how different Christians understand the relationship between 'the word of God' and the Bible:

- Is the one just a synonym for the other?
- Does the Bible 'contain' the word of God?
- Is there another, perhaps more subtle relationship between them?
- In seeking to develop Holy Habits, how does our understanding and experience shape our living?

A spectrum of opinion exists amongst Christians, and so this booklet does not give *the* definitive answer on these and other questions about the Bible – questions about which there is so much difference of opinion between honest, committed Christians. What you are asked to do is to recognise that there are honest and well-intentioned differences, and to deal with these differences in a spirit of love and humility.

Two perspectives

In order to understand something of the nature of these differences, we will reflect a little on the perspectives of two Christian denominations as examples of the kind of things churches say about the place of the Bible in the Christian faith.

The 'Basis of Union' of the United Reformed Church expresses the relationship between the word of God and the Bible in these words:

> The United Reformed Church… acknowledges the Word of God in the Old and New Testaments, discerned under the guidance of the Holy Spirit, as the supreme authority for the faith and conduct of all God's people. (Paragraph A12)

There are similarities between this and the corresponding statement of the Methodist Church in its 'Deed of Union':

> The doctrines of the evangelical faith which Methodism has held from the beginning and still holds are based upon the divine revelation recorded in the holy scriptures. The Methodist Church acknowledges this revelation as the supreme rule of faith and practice.

Reread these URC and Methodist statements carefully. What do you find that they say about:

- the holy scriptures?
- the word of God?
- God's revelation to humanity?
- the role of the Holy Spirit in relation to the Bible?

Much of the controversy about the Bible that has taken place between Christians has focused on the issue of authority. Where does authority lie? Are there safeguards against an 'anything goes' approach to the Christian faith and life? What are the foundations of our Christian faith?

A follow-up report of the Methodist Church observes that the statement in the Deed of Union 'says that the divine revelation, which is recorded in the holy scriptures, is the supreme authority for the church. It does not say that the Bible is the supreme authority' (**www.methodist.org.uk/downloads/conf-the-nature-of-authority-2001. pdf**). Compare this comment with the URC statement above: are there similarities or differences between them?

The same paragraph of the URC manual affirms that the church 'acknowledges that the life of faith to which it is called is a gift of the Holy Spirit continually received in Word and Sacrament and in the common life of God's people'. Reflect on the phrase 'the common life of God's people'. They draw our attention to the need for Christians to heed the apostle Paul's injunction, 'Do not be conformed to this world' (Romans 12:2) in the way that we read the Bible.

How does a Christian read the Bible?

Protestant Christians, especially, have at times been prone to be too influenced by the individualistic spirit of the age. This shows itself in an attitude which says in effect, 'I and my Bible can determine the full and final truth on any matter.'

We may try to moderate this attitude by adding 'With the help of the Holy Spirit, I and my Bible…' but this misses something crucial about what it means to be a Christian. The Holy Spirit is the Spirit of the body of Christ and, although we each share in the Spirit, it is only in being members of the one body that we experience the fullness of the Spirit's ministry (see 1 Corinthians 12:12–13).

What does this mean for the way we read and interpret the Bible? It means that it has to be done within 'the common life of God's people'. This is the context in which the gift of the Holy Spirit operates fully in the life of faith. That means listening humbly to the understandings of others (in home groups, in local churches), being open to what Christians of other denominations say and being open to what Christians over the two millennia of the Christian church's existence have to say.

The technical term for this wider context for our Bible reading and our theological understanding more generally is 'tradition'. Tradition in this sense has nothing to do with being 'traditional' in the popular sense of the word. Nor is it tradition in the sense which Jesus condemns (Mark 7:8). Rather, it means that we cannot operate simply as individuals; we need to recognise that as Christians we exist in a supportive relationship with other members of the body of Christ, past and present, and that this is the primary medium through which God chooses to operate. Of course, we are individually responsible for engaging with God's truth, but we cannot do that in an *individualistic* way.

Three legs or four?

Although there are differences of opinion between denominations, and between individual Christians, the place of 'tradition' in reading and interpreting scripture has always been supplemented by the inclusion of reason – with reason being understood as a God-given faculty which is used together with tradition in order to grasp the meaning of scripture. The image of a three-legged stool has been used to illustrate how these three elements – scripture, reason and tradition – have their part to play in discerning the will of God.

John Wesley, as an Anglican minister and the founder of Methodism, added a fourth element, which was discerned by Albert Outler, the leading American Methodist theologian of the 20th century; the Bible came first for Wesley, and the other three were tradition, reason and experience. It is worth noting that, although Outler coined the term 'Wesleyan Quadrilateral' to describe this fourfold approach, he came to wish that he had never used it: 'It has created the wrong image in the minds of so many people and, I am sure, will lead to all kinds of controversy' (quoted in David W. Jones, *An Introduction to Biblical Ethics*, B&H Academic, 2013, p. 19).

The problem, as Outler saw, is that the term gives the impression of four equal sides, or four legs to the chair of authority, each operating in the same way, and this is not how Wesley conceived the way these four elements relate to each other. What it does do, though, is to highlight the need to set our reading of the Bible in the wider context of tradition, as well as recognising that our God-given faculty of reason is the necessary tool by which we appropriate the truths of the Bible, and that if those truths are to be meaningful they need to be given life in our experience.

Sharing your story

Earlier in this booklet there is the story of *The Apprentice* candidate Samuel, who explained how he seeks to live his life in line with **Biblical Teaching**. You might like to reflect upon and share your stories of living out **Biblical Teaching** in small groups, in services or via social media. Could you share an online diary, video or blog post about this?

ARTS AND MEDIA

There are many films and books containing scenes about **Biblical Teaching** which could be used as an illustration in worship. However, it is suggested that the following films and books are watched or read in their entirety and followed by a discussion to go deeper into the topic of **Biblical Teaching**.

Films

God on Trial (12, 2008, 1h26m)

A group of Jews awaiting death in a concentration camp put God on trial to determine whether he has gone against his covenant with humanity.

- Which life experiences challenge our engagement with **Biblical Teaching**?
- Which parts of **Biblical Teaching** help us to deal with these challenges?

††††† The Lion, the Witch and the Wardrobe (PG, 2005, 2h23m)

Four children travel through a magical wardrobe to Narnia, where they discover their destiny to free the land from the evil White Witch, with the help of a mystical lion.

- **Biblical Teaching** is about living God's way, about living the Holy Habits. What do each of the children learn about how they live and what they do?
- How might this relate to your living out of the Holy Habits?

☺ The Matrix (15, 1999, 2h16m)

In this, the first of a series of three films, we follow the tale of Thomas Anderson, a computer hacker going under the name Neo, who discovers that the world is actually a simulated reality called the 'Matrix'. He is invited to leave the Matrix and enter the fight against the machines which have enslaved humanity for energy. It is prophesied that the 'One' will come and will overpower the machines.

- The parallels between this story and the Bible are striking, although radically different, and it is worth watching through that lens.

Noah (12A, 2014, 2h18m)

A retelling of the biblical story of Noah.

- Compare the film with the story of Noah in the Bible (Genesis 6—10). How faithful is the film to the original text?
- Are there parts of the Bible you would prefer to ignore because you find them difficult or confusing? Is there anything you wish could be added?

Philomena (12A, 2013, 1h38m)

This film is based on a true story, told in a book of the same name by Martin Sixsmith. A political journalist becomes invested in the story of a Catholic woman's search for her son, who was taken away from her after she became pregnant and was sent to a convent.

- How is **Biblical Teaching** used (or misused) to justify the actions of the different protagonists in the film?

ᛚᛚᛚᛚ The Prince of Egypt
(U, 1998, 1h39m)

This animated retelling of the story of Exodus follows the life of Moses, who, upon discovering his Hebrew slave roots, starts on a journey for God which leads him to rescue his people from bondage.

- Compare the film with the story of Moses in the Bible (Exodus). How faithful is the film to the original text?
- Are there parts of the Bible you would prefer to ignore because you find them difficult or confusing? Is there anything you wish could be added?

ᛚᛚᛚᛚ Veggie Tales

This series of children's animated films features fruit and vegetable characters. In each episode, a different Bible story is retold in a humorous way. These stories are great for primary-school-aged children.

- How could you use films – these or others – as a way of introducing children to **Biblical Teaching**?

Books: fiction

Are there people in your church or local community who would like to discuss some of these books at a book club? Guidance on how to form these is widely available online, and you could also ask denominational training officers for help.

A Lineage of Grace: Five stories of unlikely women who changed eternity
Francine Rivers (Tyndale House Publishers, 2009)

Five stories about five unlikely women in Jesus' family line who challenged and changed the world. These five women from the Bible were women of hope, faith, love and obedience who received and knew God's unlimited grace in their lives. This book is historical fiction that unpacks the Bible in a new way.

- When or where have you especially encountered God's grace?
- What scripture comes to mind when you reflect on these experiences?

The Da Vinci Code
Dan Brown (Transworld, 2003)

This story explores an alternative religious history. The central plot point is that the Merovingian kings of France were descended from the bloodline of Jesus Christ and Mary Magdalene, an idea also found in Clive Prince's *The Templar Revelation* (1997) and books by Margaret Starbird. This book was adapted into a film of the same name (12A, 2006, 2h29m).

- Are there books or films which have challenged your relationship with **Biblical Teaching**?
- How can we respond to this and similar novels?

The Neverending Story
Michael Ende (Puffin, 1983)

In the story, a young boy who is finding life lonely and difficult picks up a fantasy book and starts to read it. The characters are looking for someone to come to help them, and he gradually realises that the person they are looking for is him. He steps into the world of the story and has lots of adventures. He also grows through the experience, and eventually steps back into his normal life a changed person who is better able to deal with things and help people.

- How have you known Jesus calling you through the Bible to step into his story, and let your experience of him become part of the story of your life?

The Shadow of the Galilean
Gerd Theissen (new edition, SCM Classics, 2010)

The story of a Jewish merchant forced into spying for the Romans. He is sent to discover whether Jesus is a threat to Roman rule. The story includes a wealth of information about Palestinian life and politics, which you can follow up in the notes if you wish. There is also a series of letters between Theissen and another scholar about the pluses and minuses of writing a book like this. But you can ignore those until you have read the story!

How can a broader understanding of biblical times help our engagement with **Biblical Teaching**?

Books: non-fiction

Bible and Mission: Christian witness in a postmodern world
Richard Bauckham (Baker Academic, 2004)

An engaging study which provides a new way of looking at scripture and that takes seriously the biblical idea of mission in the contemporary world.

- How does your perspective on scripture impact on your mission as a Christian in the world today?

Defenceless Flower: A new reading of the Bible
Carlos Mesters (Orbios, 1989/2006)

A fascinating series of chapters exploring the importance of the Bible in the growing Christian 'liberation' communities in Latin America.

- What can you learn about how the Bible might speak to you from the experience of South American Christian communities?

Introduction to Biblical Studies
Steve Moyise (second edition, T&T Clark, 2004)

This book gives a fascinating introduction to a vast range of approaches to the Bible.

- Which of the approaches outlined in this book challenge you to understand the Bible in new ways?

Scripture and the Authority of God
Tom Wright (revised and expanded edition, SPCK, 2013)

In this book, Tom Wright demonstrates the indispensable role of scripture as the primary resource for teaching and guidance in the Christian life. It includes two helpful case studies, looking at what it means to keep the sabbath and at how Christians can defend marital monogamy, and offering bold biblical insights about them.

- How does what Tom Wright says about the Bible and the authority of God relate to other crucial issues in contemporary society?

Telling the Bible: Over 100 stories to read aloud
Bob Hartman (Monarch Books, 2006)

Bringing the Bible to life in a memorable way for adults and children by storytelling. The stories can be read aloud in worship, house groups, schools and other settings.

Each story is accompanied by useful 'Telling Tips' to help enhance the experience.

- Can biblical storytelling augment **Biblical Teaching** in a way that establishes the Holy Habit more effectively?

Why Read the Bible?
Tom Wright (SPCK, 2015)

A little book of guidance on the contents, inspiration, meaning and authority of the Bible for anyone looking for easy ways into the topic.

- What might Tom Wright's account of the inspiration and authority of the Bible add to your own understanding of the nature and purpose of the Bible?

The Year of Living Biblically
A.J. Jacobs (Arrow, 2009)

One person's spiritual journey as he attempts to obey every rule in the Bible – especially the less-publicised ones. This book can be a little facetious in places but it raises significant questions about what it might mean for Christians to base their lives on the Bible.

- What questions about your own use of the Bible does this book raise for you?

Articles and online media

Good News Stories

- St John's Stone (**youtu.be/ QJdPqFf3fOQ** or search YouTube for 'Good News Stories with Nick').
- Oakengates Goes Eco-Church (**youtu.be/KTs--fi6jCE** or search YouTube for 'Good News Stories with Nick').

A Word in Time

A Word in Time (**www.methodist. org.uk/prayer-and-worship/a-word-in-time**) suggests a Bible passage to read each day, and gives some helpful thoughts and pointers to your own reflections about it. There is a facility for looking at other people's reactions to the passage and adding your own.

Navigate

The 'Navigate' resource for children and young people contains a number of short introductory video clips, answering questions such as:

- Why should I read the Bible?
- How do I read it?
- What difference does the Bible make?

All videos and session plans are available for free at **www.methodist. org.uk/navigate**.

Music

The following song may help you to explore and reflect further on this habit.

The Light
The Proclaimers

Poetry

A number of poems are referenced below. Choose one to reflect on.

You may wish to consider some of the following questions:

- What does this poem say to you about **Biblical Teaching**?
- Which images do you find helpful or unhelpful?
- How is your practice of **Biblical Teaching** challenged by this poem?
- Could you write a poem to share with others the virtues of **Biblical Teaching**?

Haiku Beatitudes: 10 songs for a new world
Ian Adams, from *Unfurling* (Canterbury Press, 2015)

The Lectern
Malcolm Guite, from *Sounding the Seasons* (Canterbury Press, 2012)

Temptations 1: Stones into bread
Malcolm Guite, from *Sounding the Seasons* (Canterbury Press, 2012)

Christ Writes in the Dust – the Woman Taken in Adultery

Clive Hicks-Jenkins (b. 1951): acrylic on panel, 2011, 82 x 62 cm.
From the Methodist Modern Art Collection, © TMCP, used with permission.
You can download this image from: www.methodist.org.uk/artcollection

The artist, formerly a choreographer, stage director and designer, depicts the story of John 8:1–11 at the point where Christ distracts the crowd's attention from the accused woman by writing in the dust. The artist has commented, 'I decided to use mirror images… their shapes almost interlocking.' The background is based on sketches of Montclar in Catalonia, a picturesque village visited by the artist in 2010.

- The painting was commissioned in order to demonstrate the readiness of Jesus to stand against, or go beyond, much Old Testament teaching. How does the painting evoke this?
- This is a narrative painting, which the artist intended to be 'an exploration, in the process of which revelations may occur'. Does the painting speak to you in this way?
- How does the image speak to you of **Biblical Teaching**?
- Can you draw or paint a picture evoking an aspect of **Biblical Teaching**?

Footprints

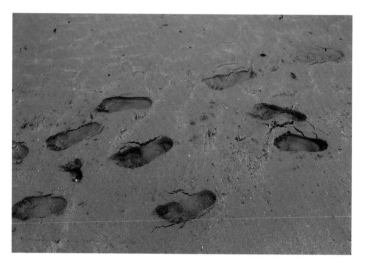

What Bible passages does this picture call to mind?

The 'Footprints in the Sand' prayer may be familiar – two sets of footprints through life but only one through the difficult times, when God carries us. What is the impact of **Biblical Teaching** for individuals, for congregations, for society, for nations?

Biblical Teaching might be seen to include commandments and promises. Reflect on Psalm 119:35–133.

Credits

In addition to the Holy Habits editorial/development team, contributions to this booklet also came from: Eddy Aigbe, Linda Bates, Gill Day, Brian Dickens, Rachel Frank, Dorothy Graham, Ken Howcroft, Becca Lees, Vincent Jambawo, Graham Lowe, Tony Malcolm, Andrew Mason, Tony McClelland, Sarah Middleton, Tom Milton, Pause for Thought at Dorridge Methodist Church, Perry Hall Youth Group (including Nicholas Greaves, Benjamin Heagren, Esther Humphries, Rebekah Humphries, Alexis Johnson, Chloe Sutton), Helen Pollard, Marjorie Roper, Sparkhill Bible Study Group, Karen Webber and Helen Woodall.

'This set of ten resources will enable churches and individuals to begin to establish "habits of faithfulness". In the United Reformed Church, we are calling this process of developing discipleship, "Walking the Way: Living the life of Jesus today" and I have no doubt that this comprehensive set of resources will enable us to do just that.'
Revd Richard Church, Deputy General Secretary (Discipleship), United Reformed Church

'Here are some varied and rich resources to help further deepen our discipleship of Christ, encouraging and enabling us to adopt the life-transforming habits that make for following Jesus.'
Revd Dr Martyn Atkins, Team Leader & Superintendent Minister, Methodist Central Hall, Westminster

'The Holy Habits resources will help you, your church, your fellowship group, to engage in a journey of discovery about what it really means to be a disciple today. I know you will be encouraged, challenged and inspired as you read and work your way through each chapter. There is lots to study together and pray about, and that can only be good as our churches today seek to bring about the kingdom of God.'
Revd Loraine Mellor, President of the Methodist Conference 2017/18

'The Holy Habits resources help weave the spiritual through everyday life. They're a great tool that just get better with use. They help us grow in our desire to follow Jesus as their concern is formation not simply information.'
Olive Fleming Drane and John Drane

'The Holy Habits resources are an insightful and comprehensive manual for living in the way of Jesus in the 21st century: an imaginative, faithful and practical gift for the church that will sustain and invigorate our life and mission in a demanding world. The Holy Habits resources are potentially transformational for a church.'
Revd Ian Adams, Mission Spirituality Adviser for Church Mission Society

'To understand the disciplines of the Christian life without practising them habitually is like owning a fine collection of soap but never having a wash. The team behind Holy Habits knows this, which is why they have produced these excellent and practical resources. Use them, and by God's grace you will grow in holiness.'
Paul Bayes, Bishop of Liverpool

'The Holy Habits resources are a rich mine of activities for all ages to help change minds, attitudes and behaviours. I love the way many different people groups are represented and celebrated, and the constant references to the complex realities of 21st-century life.'
Lucy Moore, Founder of BRF's Messy Church